Chris Langrish lives on his family farm in Hampshire with his two grown children, James and Emily, and his three dogs, Willow, Patch, and Larry. He recently retired from a twenty-five-year career as a lecturer in Performing Arts at Chichester College in West Sussex. He originally trained as an actor at the Birmingham School of Speech Training and Dramatic Art, graduating in 1988. This is his first book.

This book is dedicated to Lindsay.

Chris Langrish

A GRIEF OBSERVED

AUSTIN MACAULEY PUBLISHERS
LONDON * CAMBRIDGE * NEW YORK * SHARJAH

Copyright © Chris Langrish 2025

The right of Chris Langrish to be identified as author of this work has been asserted by the author in accordance with sections 77 and 78 of the Copyright, Designs and Patents Act 1988.

All rights reserved. No part of this publication may be reproduced, stored in a retrieval system, or transmitted in any form or by any means, electronic, mechanical, photocopying, recording, or otherwise, without the prior permission of the publishers.

Any person who commits any unauthorised act in relation to this publication may be liable to criminal prosecution and civil claims for damages.

A CIP catalogue record for this title is available from the British Library.

ISBN 9781035893430 (Paperback)
ISBN 9781035893447 (ePub e-book)

www.austinmacauley.com

First Published 2025
Austin Macauley Publishers Ltd®
1 Canada Square
Canary Wharf
London
E14 5AA

James & Emily Langrish And our three dogs Willow, Patch and Larry

Thanks to Simon Higlett for the drawings and Richard Paterson for the photographs

1. **GREY**
    Shall I visit her grave on the greyest of days?
    Shall I lay flowers on the spot where she lays?
    The leaves are falling from the trees
    And everywhere feels grey.

2. **FOG**
    We miss you, quietly, but crying at night.
    Sniffles in supermarkets
    And tears walking dogs.
    Wearing dark sunglasses in mid-winter fogs.

3. **REMEMBER**
    Remember her, but try not to dwell.
    Remember the days when things seemed so swell.
    Remember slow love in the late afternoon?
    A stroll on the beach under the moon.
    Dancing and partying,
    Dinner with friends
    Laughter and giggling
    Who thought it would end.

4. **WINDOW**

   I can feel you and sense you about in our room.
   A feeling you're here, but it all goes too soon.
   The stillness and quiet now you're not there.
   I sit by our window; I sit and I stare.

5. **MORNING**

   I sit in the morning sun and I think of you.
   I look up towards the sky, and it's pure blue.
   I sit in the morning sun, but what should I do?
   The whole day ahead of me,
   But without you.

6. **CANOPY**

   I walk under the green canopy sometimes crying.
   Last year's fallen leaves beneath my feet,
   From the time when you were dying.
   The dogs scamper and play ahead of me.
   They don't feel my pain.
   They live every day as it comes,
   With everything to gain.

7. **BLACKBERRY**
   The season changes from green leaf to rust.
   The grave mound slowly sinks
   From flesh to inevitable dust.
   I pick the blackberries sweet to the taste.
   The days, weeks, and months
   Pass me by without haste.

8. **24 DAYS**
   Twenty-four days from health to death.
   For twenty-four days the cancer spread its lethal breath.
   You left work early one late afternoon.
   Called me to say, "Can you come home soon?
   I don't feel too good. The dogs needing walking and then a feed."
   "Yes, of course." I said, "Where's the lead?"

   Twenty-four days in the hospital, then hospice bed.
   The doctors ring one early morn.
   "The results are in. Can you come straight away?"
   "It's terminal, we're sorry to say."
   I look to her and hold her hand
   And I silently pray.

9. **BABY STEPS**
   Would have, could have, should have.
   These thoughts will make me mad.
   The things we could have done together,
   Oh, I wish we had.
   No point living in regret,

Or dwelling on the past.
Take baby steps towards my future,
But be careful, not too fast.

10. COME BACK

Come back to me so we can talk.
Come back to me
Let's go for a walk.
Discuss our future plans and what to do
For me and you.

11. SUN SETS

I thought we would grow old together
Sitting in the garden watching the sun set.
Taking mid-afternoon naps
And bouncing grandchildren on our laps.

I thought we would grow old together
But now it's not to be.
I thought you'd be by my side forever
Just you and me.

12. A FEELING

I sense you in the autumn breeze
A glint of sun behind a cloud.
Your body gone, but not your soul.
You're with me here right now.

13. WARDROBE

Your dresses are in the wardrobe
Your shoes are in the hall.
Your perfume and hairbrush are on the dresser
Where you left it all.
Shampoo left in the shower
Dressing robe hanging on the door.
Slippers tucked under our bed
On the bedroom floor.

14. WATERLOO

I know that eventually I must move on from you.
But you do appreciate that it's hard for me to do.
The history that we had is impossible to replicate.
We met under the clock at Waterloo
You saw me, and I saw you.

15. SUNDAY

Sunday is a difficult day to get through.
Sundays are hard without you.
Like Sundays from childhood that weren't much fun.
The whole day stretches ahead of me.
Till the setting of the sun.

16. PLEASE GOD

Twelve months, a whole year since you left me.
We've carried on the best we could, the kids and me.
If only we could see you again
To ease our collective pain.
If only you could be risen from the dead.
We could hear your laughter

See your smile.
Oh, please, God, can you?
Just for a little while.

17. BREZZE
You're in the wind and in the breeze.
I feel you with the rustle of the leaves.
You're everywhere I go
Though not in the physical form, I know.
But you're with me as always, just the same
As if we were walking hand in hand
Down our lane.

18. ONE FOR THE ROAD
I suggest one more for the road
But he looks towards the clock
Replies, I'd love to, but I better not.
I'd love to stay, but there'll be hell to pay.
He has a wife to go back to
And I do not.

19. COULD I?

Could I start a new chapter and move forward with my life?
Oh, I do hope so,
Perhaps someday soon.
Could I turn the page at last,
Instead of looking back continually to the past?
Could I plan a future with new
Love
Joy
Laughter
Tears
Could I look to the future
With nothing to fear?

20. ON THE DAY YOU DIED

You were quiet and shy
And never made much fuss.
The moment you passed, I was looking at my phone
I looked up to see you, but you didn't moan
Quietly and gently, your breathing just ceased.
They hung a paper butterfly on the hospice room door
To inform others to give us some peace
I knelt by your bed and took your hand
And after a while, carefully removed your wedding band.

21.

The house is a little shabbier since you passed
Cobwebs lurking in the corners
And dust on picture frames

Dog hair stuck to sofas
Dried mud on the tiled floor.
The plants in their pots have withered and died
I had promised you I'd water them
So sorry that I lied.
New doors in the living room
The garden wall finally complete
I've tried to cut the grass to keep it short and neat .

22.

The silence in the house is sometimes hard to bear
Not that you were ever noisy
But you're no longer there.
The ping on my phone
To say you are almost home
The barking of the dogs
Mad for a bone.
"How was your day, darling?"
I used to ask
But now silence
I'm all alone.

23.

    Our friends have been very kind to me
    Just thought you'd like to know
    Bike rides
    Barbecues
    Coffee and cakes
    And walks around the lake.
    I'm always included with kindness and care
    Now that you my darling girl
    Are no longer there.

24.

    The moments of silence we shared,
    We liked doing nothing together
    We didn't care.
    Our friends rushing from here to there
    Perpetual motion from dawn to dusk
    We would just sit and smile at each other
    And thought, *What's all the fuss?*

25.

    I found a frozen dinner tucked at the back of the fridge
    A handwritten note by you stuck to the lid: *Here's a chicken curry, in case you're in a hurry.*
    xx.

26. MUM

    The children don't mention you very much.
    Their grief is private, hidden from view.
    Alone in their bedrooms, they think of you.

Their mum, mother, confidant, and friend
The parent who was patient with them to the end
Would hear what they had to say
And offer her advice in a calm, measured way.

27. DON'T WISH IT ALL AWAY

Were you happy in our marriage?
Content with your life?
Should I have paid less attention
To the trouble and the strife?

Make the most of the day
You used to say
Try not to wish it all away
Let the kids build dens with the sheets
On the living room floor
I know you're tired from work the day before
But don't shout or be irritable
Let them have fun
Let them have their time in the sun.

28. FINSBURY PARK TUBE

I used to meet you at the top of Finsbury Park tube
Watch you ascend from the depths below
Wearing John Lennon glasses, Doc Marten boots
And awkward student clothes
A shy girl from Rhode Island State
Studying in London as part of your degree
How lucky we were that we met
And that you fell in love with me

29. TEA

Can you see us walking in the woods, the dogs and me?
Oh, I wish you could be with us; how happy you would be
We always said the simple things in life are best
Walks
Strolls
Damp dogs
And steaming cups of tea.